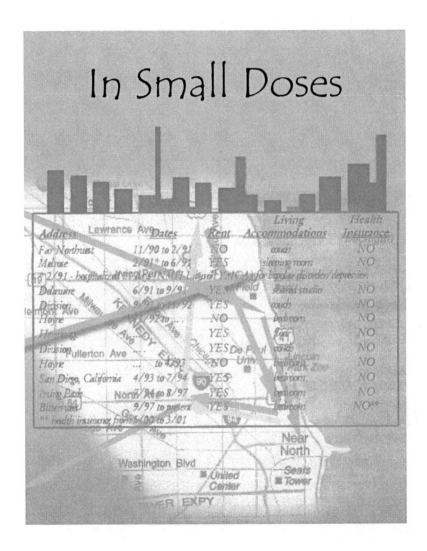

In Small Doses

A Memoir about Accepting and Living
with Bipolar Disorder

MARC POLLARD

Near North Press

Library of Congress Control Number: 2003110030

ISBN: 1-56550-092-X

Cover art by Jay Anson

Book Design by Illumination Graphics
Grants Pass, Oregon
www.illuminationgraphics.com

Published by Near North Press
Chicago, Illinois
niche@nearnorthpress.com
www.insmalldoseshome.com
Printed in U.S.A.

First Edition

CONTENTS

INTRODUCTION

This memoir takes the reader on a journey as old as a quarter of a century, retracing the harrowing, bittersweet experiences of the author, an adult manic-depressive with a long, fiercely guarded history of childhood depression. In small doses, an evolving "working model" of bipolar disorder begins to emerge while resistance toward diagnosis and medication compliance slowly wears away. The decision to present the subject in an anecdotal fashion reflects the author's attempt to keep the reader both uniformed and misinformed. In this way, the reader's understanding of bipolar disorder should mimic that of the author's.

Along the way, the reader is confronted with a broad array of social issues. Foremost among them are childhood depression and its treatment. Other issues that come to the fore range from the potential dangers that arise when "treating" bipolar disorder with the 12 Steps of Alcoholics Anonymous alone, to a society that abhors mental illness yet is incapable of recognizing its socially acceptable manifestations[1], to a health care system that works to exclude the treatment of mental illness (considered inessential), and finally, to financial calamity arising from the combination of debt, underemployment, relative unemployability, and, predictably, bankruptcy.

---

[1] It is estimated that over 17.4 million adults in the U.S. suffer from an affective (mood) disorder each year – that comes to one out of every seven people (National Depressive and Manic-Depressive Association).

ACKNOWLEDGEMENTS

Among the reasons I have for writing this book is the desire to express my deepest gratitude to those individuals who have made my life, not always thought worth living, worthwhile. So with that, I'd like to thank Jeff Walls, Michelle Greene, Keith Ross, and Dr. Joan Leska. I'd also like to thank the wonderful people who staff the community mental health centers who have helped me so much over the years. And finally, with the aid of psychiatric hospital personnel, I have learned that a psychiatric hospital isn't the worst place one can find oneself.

PROLOGUE

My first attempt to migrate was thwarted by my family and something called Alcoholics Anonymous. At the time I was relieved to have some relatively benign, albeit crude, "diagnosis" that might account for the living hell I called my life. Only a week before I had surrendered all of my savings and credit, including the principle from a large personal loan, to a church that I knew nothing about with designs on working as a missionary in the Far East. To get to the Far East, however, I first had to purchase a "bridge" from a church pitchman. Upon reviewing my credentials (I had a good paying job, I was an excellent credit risk, I was willing, and, most of all, I was sitting right there in front of him), the salesman announced that I had in fact received a "scholarship" from the church. In effect, this meant that the sum of my savings, credit, and personal loan had to total $12,000. Confused? Would you believe that the twelve grand changed hands in less than twenty minutes, with virtually no questions asked? Who, you might ask, would do such a thing? Well, I, for one, would. To assist you in constructing a profile of someone who would do such a thing, I have included the following table (next page) containing demographic information about myself.

This profile didn't helped at all, did it? Can you imagine what factors might have led me to walk away from my American Dream – possessions, career, friends, and even family? Got it yet? Well, perhaps you will come to understand after embarking on this vicarious migration into the "wilderness." Be forewarned, however, the footing is extremely treacherous and often unstable. After all, you, the reader, will be making this trek in the shoes of the mentally ill.

All of the mythology and clichés born of Americana apply. Mine is the tale of the quintessential All-American boy, a success story in the making in pursuit of the American

Table 1. Demographic Data About the Author

Age: 22
Sex: Male
Race: Caucasian

SES: Middle to upper-middle class; born, raised, and educated in affluent San Francisco Bay Area; employed as an analyst in economic consulting (first job out of college, 1988; $30,000 salary)

Education: Bachelors in science, concentration in economics; admitted to Ph.D. program in economics; recipient of Proctor & Gamble Fellowship in Economics, 1989 ($10,000 stipend, tuition waived)

Other: Star athlete, football (captain) and track and field; national high school scholar-athlete, recipient of $1,000 "student-athlete" scholarship; one year of college football (JV/captain)

Dream. It is also the story of a life that seemingly "slipped through the cracks." I have one tragic flaw you see, one hamartia. Unbeknownst to me and, more importantly, to those around me, I am bipolar. Unfortunately, this is not something that is stamped on one's forehead at birth and typically is not diagnosed until one reaches one's twenties. Moreover, anyone oblivious to the subject of mental illness, morbidly fearful of being flawed, and prone to literal interpretation of the Bible or one's religious tenants when all else fails, might come to understand my situation from these facts:

✳ My family doctor said that there aren't any fitter than me, my parents said that I amazed them, my coaches and teammates named me captain of every team, and academicians at every level sang my praises.

✳ The mental anguish and despair I experienced were both recurrent and increasing in intensity.

✳ I knew that there was something terribly wrong with me, yet I was caught up in a charade that surely could not go on forever.

✳ I thought I must be a horrible person because God was punishing me.

Conclusion: *I'm better off dead.*

Chapter 1
MIGRATION

I've considered it for sometime, yet I'm still here? Am I
really going to kill myself? Probably not. And the way
I've gone about it up to this point is simply taking too
long. So, it appears that I'm going to stick around a lot
longer than I would like. If that's the case, then I want
out. I want to disappear. Yes, I will offer the world this
compromise. In exchange for suicide, I will disappear.

As it turns out, what the church pitchman sold me was simply a little more time. Besides, what's twelve thousand dollars to Bill Gates or the utterly hopeless? I did not stick
around the church long enough to voyage overseas, however. Instead, at my father's suggestion, I began attending the

meetings of Alcoholics Anonymous. Alcoholism had become an easy, blanket diagnosis for those oblivious to psychiatry and psychology. Count my family, myself, and everyone that I have ever known or met among them. Suffice it to say that untreated psychiatric disorders are simply beyond the scope of Alcoholics Anonymous.

Of course... I have problems every time I drink; my drinking is noticeably different from those around me. I drink to get drunk; my behavior becomes wildly out-of-control, dangerous, and promiscuous; the social impact of my drinking is devastating; the personal toll from my drinking is great.

Interestingly, the only question that I could not respond to in the affirmative, the alcoholics neglected to ask: "Have you ever seen a psychiatrist?"

A.A. is a mixed bag for all who attend; it just happens to be a bit too mixed for the mentally ill. The principles upon which the program is founded are sound, the 12 Steps themselves are noble. The meetings, which allow members to share their experience, strength, and hope with one another certainly helped me break through my protracted silence. Finally, the concept of the support group is a significant contribution to modern society, in general, and to the mentally ill, in particular, who are often separated from their friends, families, and society for various reasons. Unfortunately, the principles upon which Alcoholics Anonymous were founded are both incomplete and subject to interpretation by uninformed and misinformed human beings.

Rather than disappearing to the Far East, I resigned to becoming a "good A.A." Inexplicably, within 30-days I had metamorphosed into a somewhat ostentatious recovering alcoholic with a message: "all praise and glory goes to God and Alcoholics Anonymous." In this instance, this was a truly ominous statement. When discussing bipolar disorder, it is worth noting that the 12 Steps were brilliantly conceived (by an individual whose own mood swings are well documented) in such a way that, by working the simple program, one begins to feel better about themselves, in some cases, immediately. Unfortunately, things just go haywire when the recovering alcoholic happens to be an undiagnosed manic-depressive.

Someone more prudent might have deferred their amends to an unspecified later date. Not me. I had recently been admitted to graduate school at the University of Illinois and was down to my final thirty days in California. I was not planning on returning to make amends. Besides, everything, including amends making and check writing, comes easily to the zealot. During July 1989, I wrote checks in excess of $1,600 as part of my amends. That torrid 20-day love affair set me back the price of a modest diamond ring ($250) and hotel accommodations for a get-away weekend in Lake Tahoe, California (another $250). And lastly, I paid my disabled A.A. sponsor's rent for one month ($800). This was not a loan. I didn't expect to see this money again. My expectations were correct. This was an act of gratitude, for I believed that the man had truly saved my life. Besides, what's another eight hundred bucks to the hopelessly delirious?

Within weeks of my move to Illinois, my first A.A. sponsor explained that he was not doing very well shortly before disappearing. My guess is that he relapsed, which recovering alcoholics are known to do. I would account for his relapse as not due to any fault of his own. More likely, it seemed that my whirlwind, summer-long, manic episode was so powerfully intoxicating that it simply engulfed him, too. To this day, he's probably wondering what the hell happened, where had he gone wrong? Poor man.

In any event, I spent the next two very long and tumultuous, but sober years in and out of Alcoholics Anonymous, in and out of graduate school, and in and out of society.

> Seen your case before. Started getting cocky, then you were gone. Happens all the time. We knew you'd come back with your tail between your legs. This time, you are going to work the steps the right way.

Seen my case before? Quite frankly, I'm sure that the alcoholics had, many times before. After all, there is considerable comorbidity between bipolar disorder and alcoholism (or other forms of substance abuse, for that matter). Regrettably, alcoholism was the only diagnosis I had at this point. Also regrettably, the 12 Steps alone could not treat bipolar disorder. Bipolar disorder requires both medication (a dirty word to some members of A.A.) to stabilize one's profound mood swings, and psychotherapy, to attempt to give meaning to the bits and fragments in utter chaos that one conventionally labels a life.

Now that my life had been spared, the summer's end meant the start of my curious migration. In the spring of 1989, I had been admitted as a Ph.D. candidate to study economics at the University of Illinois, located a little more than two thousand miles east, in central Illinois. Remarkably, within days of receiving notice of a fellowship award and tuition waiver, I had purchased a "bridge" to the Far East from a church salesman in hopes of disappearing. But that was April and this was July, and the American Dream had returned to its R.E.M. state. And so, with both feet frenetically darting in every direction, I boarded a train with a one-way ticket to the Midwest.

Initially, the fellowship of Alcoholics Anonymous played a major role in my efforts to integrate into my new community. Prior to leaving California, I had contacted the A.A. service office in Champaign, Illinois to let them know the date and time my train was due in – about 1:00 a.m. When I arrived, closer to 3:00 a.m., I was greeted by four strangers, all recovering alcoholics holding signs baring my name. And just like that, I had an instant support group. Before long, I was deeply entrenched in the same fellowship that I had left behind.

Having doled out nearly $3,000 over the previous 30 days, however, I arrived in Champaign completely broke and met with a bank officer to obtain a short-term loan until my stipend kicked-in. That was about the time that those handy little pre-approved credit cards started showing up in droves. *Hell yes, I'm an excellent credit risk! I'm working on my Ph.D. in economics – I'm going to be rolling in dough, someday.* Remarkably, as time passed and as I had gotten further and further removed from the semblance of a legitimate career, I would happen upon this constant. I never had to be enrolled in any graduate program, working toward anything in particular, or even working at all to recognize what the credit card companies thought they'd surmised long ago. Not only was I an excellent credit risk, but someday I'd be rolling in dough!

Little did I know then that I'd be getting those pre-approved credit cards long after filing for bankruptcy and months since making a single credit card payment.

By the start of my first semester of graduate school, I was completely enraptured. Not coincidentally, I also discovered that I had outgrown A.A. In short, I found myself disgusted with those who weren't more like me; i.e., fearlessly attacking recovery so as to live, as suggested by Alcoholics Anonymous' main text, happy, joyous, and free. *Recovery doesn't have to be some self-imposed sentence!* In the end, I got tired of being a bad example for others: "If you behave like him, or go where he goes, you'll end up drunk." Though I wasn't afraid of life, I was brutally critical of those who were. Fortunately, I did realize early on that, unlike the others, sobriety was not an issue for me. I was truly grateful to be rid of alcohol and have never considered returning to it in all of these (twelve) years. So with that, I dropped out of A.A. less than six months after my first meeting.

My home in Champaign was a graduate dorm inhabited, about four-to-one, by international students. Fittingly, I dressed in technicolor – a lot of neon and pastels – and walked about the echoing halls in loud, flip-flop sandals. And despite all of that, I was immensely popular. The international students took to me right away, and I to them. To a large extent, much of the information they received about Americana was funneled through me. Within weeks, a lovely young French woman, Christine, had moved into my shoebox-sized dorm room. Life seemed perfectly enchanting.

By November, however, all that had changed. My internal computer had shut down. No matter how furious I typed on the keyboard, nothing was being sent to R.A.M. Sickeningly, I had felt it coming on for about two weeks. Then one day the fire was gone, extinguished and replaced by a dense fog. My time in the light had run its course. Remember, at this point I was merely an alcoholic. I had absolutely no idea what is going on inside my brain. To make matters worse, my working model had not changed significantly since childhood:

I am an awful person, I have done something unforgivable and God is punishing me. I turned my back on A.A. after they had saved my life. I got cocky and jumped into a relationship, just as they said I would. I need out! I need to drop out of my program lest they find out about me. What do I do with poor Christine? She has to go. And my dear friends? I can't let them see me like this. They, too, must go.

Though I didn't realize it at the time, Christine was the first to describe my mood swings. She had lived with me through a full cycle. Incredibly, she found this to be an endearing quality of mine. She explained that she had had her pick of men, and that her choice came down to me or Marcos, a Brazilian with a wonderful job back home, finishing his masters' thesis in electrical engineering. She chose me because, "He's too stable. His mood is constant and his career is well established – it's so boring. You are not. I picked you because you are much more uncertain. You are much more alive!" Although I was listening then, it took me about twelve years to hear what Christine was saying. At the time, however, I found her as disturbed as me. Sorry about calling the police to have you removed from my dorm room, Christine.

Now a disgraced graduate school dropout, and thousands of miles from home, I metamorphosed into a recluse on campus, avoiding everyone in my dorm. If cornered, I would avoid accounting for myself. I would say anything and nothing all at once, stare past so as not to engage, force a painfully awkward smile, and nod agreeably. In other words, my modus operandi was to get the hell out of there!

As predicted, my tail was tucked firmly between my legs when I returned to A.A. in hopes of recapturing the fire I had since lost. Here's a point, however, that was completely discounted. I hadn't relapsed. But the alcoholics had insights about me that I hadn't before considered because I shared many of the same character defects that alcoholics claimed. Besides, at the time, my working model of mental illness included these observations: *mental illness was a dreadful, institutionalized fate, the stuff of "Cuckoo's Nest," and the like. Mental illness did not afflict someone considered by all a success story.* So, back to the powder keg I went. Treat a hopeless manic-depressive with the 12 Steps alone and produce instantaneous euphoria.

My new sponsor had introduced me to the work of John Bradshaw, a family systems specialist popular at the end of the 1980s and early 1990s. By March, both my sponsor and I were convinced that I was the second coming of Bradshaw. A university professor himself, my sponsor had encouraged me to re-enroll at the graduate college. The curriculum that seemed best suited to me at this particular time was Human Development and Family Studies. So I arranged to speak with everyone in the department of about five, including the department chair, and simply channeled one response after another until all were satisfied that I was a bona fide candidate for their program. Even the top experts in their respective fields can misinterpret mania as conviction. Immunologists are no exception.

Having been admitted to the program by March, I was able to remain in the graduate dorm, though technically not a student for another six months. Six more months of career objectives to contemplate, credit card debt to grow, more student loans to go with those that I had accumulated as an undergraduate student, underemployment, and the return of an incredibly bright future resurrecting my earlier conclusion that not only was I an excellent credit risk, but someday I'd be rolling in dough!

Already a self-proclaimed family systems expert, my first task was to initiate an all-out affront on the institution of family. Where better to start than with my own. It began, as I recall writing, with a wrecking ball dressed up as an essay – a total indictment of my family of origin. Poor family. Next, I championed my anti-family movement at the tables of Alcoholics Anonymous. Again, I soon grew critical of my recovering brethren, including my sponsor, who weren't more like me – dauntlessly attacking their codependency and family of origin issues.

"Why are we pretending codependency is only the Al-Anon's problem? We all are horribly codependent, yet we act otherwise. As a result, codependency has become a dirty word around here."

In the end, I got tired of attacking these people who seemed to take comfort in hiding their codependency behind the cloak of alcoholism, as if it were a far worse indignity to be called a codependent than to be called an alcoholic. Once again I stopped showing up at Alcoholics Anonymous meetings, but this time for good.

After my family and A.A., relationships became the third and final vehicle through which I championed my movement. The predominant characteristic that defined my next three relationships, which spanned a decade from 1990 to 2000, was the rescuer-victim dynamic. In short, I saw it my duty to rescue my significant other from her oppressive, victimizing family of origin.

Before jumping to conclusions regarding my newfound role, consider that nothing I did was long lasting. Thus, in small doses I am seen, virtually by all, as extremely likeable. Viewing my public life as fragmented rather than as a continuum, the public only saw the best of me. I even controlled the information my friends received about me. I would completely disappear for an extended period of time (concurring with depression), only to reappear as the person they had originally met and known me to be – fun, vivacious, and outrageous – lest anyone suspect that something was terribly wrong. "Hey, good ol' Marc is back!"

On the other hand, too much exposure to me and I became annoying beyond belief. So, by some unconscious design, I simply was not around the same people long enough for anyone to detect a pattern. By now, any semblance of a life was long gone. I had been reduced to a human Watergate, and, like President Nixon, cover up had became an all-consuming obsession. Inevitably, when it was my time to go, I lashed out: *That's quite all right. I'm not going to waste any more of my valuable time on a bunch as pathetic as you!* In this way, I proceeded to torment one unsuspecting soul after another.

By May 1990, I was feeling quite full of myself. Not coincidentally, I was dating a young law student from Chicago. Characteristically, I was quite dazzling that summer and captivated both this young woman and her mother, alike. I can only imagine that my hyperactivity and uncanny flamboyance were like a breath of fresh crystal methamphetamine to these rather traditional, Midwestern folk. But by mid-October, the thought, *I'll never finish the semester – it was all going away, it was all over*, had returned. As the date of my oral presentation neared, I was reunited with the resolution, my one constant companion since childhood, that *I'm better off dead*. For the second time in twelve months I found myself dropping out of graduate school.

I suppose that throughout history people have migrated to Chicago for any number of reasons. To find better paying jobs, to escape slavery and the South, or to become the problem of an unsuspecting family. Of the three, I chose the latter (see Diagram 1) placing myself at the far northwest side of Chicago in November of 1990, at the residence of my girlfriend's family. Keep in mind, as my vocation was rather disruptive to traditional family life, this arrangement was doomed to fail acrimoniously. In the meantime, I was able to squeeze in another major depressive episode. Though lacking the suicidal ideation of previous episodes, the occurrence proved to be the granddaddy of them all.

Assuredly, like all Proctor & Gamble Fellowship recipients nationwide, my first job out of graduate school paid minimum wage, though mine wasn't actually entry level in my field. At the time, I was barely able to function well enough to bag groceries and push shopping carts around a parking lot the size of two football fields placed side-by-side. It was now the start of the relatively severe winter of 1990-91. Interestingly, winter is no match for profound depression. *I might be from California, but I can't feel a thing. I'm already numb.*

What I recall most about that winter is watching the Gulf War prone, from the basement couch, thinking, *soon, nobody will even notice that I'm here. I'm practically part of the furniture, already.* I also remember my girlfriend's mother and brother trying to encourage me to get up. I also remember one of them suggesting that I go to a hospital. *A hospital? Funny, hospitals are for sick people. You know, maybe I'm sick! Maybe there is something wrong with me. Never would have thought that in a hundred years.*

Would you mind participating in our research, Mr. Pollard? "No." Complete these forms and return them to me. "O.K." This is an intelligence test, Mr. Pollard. "O.K." You will be timed. "O.K." Begin now. Time, Mr. Pollard. "I couldn't finish, I know I'm not this dumb or dense. It's just that when I'm like this, I can't concentrate or think. I scored 1200 on the G.R.E." Mr. Pollard, my opinion is that you are bipolar. *I'm sorry, did you say something significant?* Bipolar disorder was once referred to as manic-depression. *I wish I could appreciate what you are telling me, but this little interview appears to be a waste of time.* Bipolar disorder occurs in about 1 percent of the population and is characterized by alternating euphoria and profound depression. Mr. Pollard, what you are experiencing now is severe depression. Mr. Pollard, I recommend you be hospitalized, immediately. *Really? Hospitalized? I wish this guy would tell me what the hell's wrong with me. Do I have cancer, a brain tumor? What, for crying out loud!* How do you feel about that, Mr. Pollard? "O.K." Mr. Pollard, I'm going to continue to see you three times a week, every Monday, Wednesday, and Friday morning. Would that be O.K. with you, Mr. Pollard? "Yes." I also recommend starting you on an antidepressant and a mood stabilizer, immediately. How do you feel about that, Mr. Pollard? "I'm a recovering alcoholic. I can't accept medication – it undermines the integrity of my recovery program."

Medication had long been considered a crutch around some tables of Alcoholics Anonymous. Despite the fact that I had severed my ties with A.A. almost a year before, I still remained determined to gain recognition as a "good A.A." and to practice their principles in all my affairs. Medication, therefore, was out of the question. And my doctor, now at the top of his field, had heard all of this pious, mumbo-jumbo long before.

Thus was my introduction to bipolar disorder. Half of everything my doctor told me about my illness rang true – the half about depression being a bad thing. The rest seemed to be projection, merely the sentiments of a quiet, mild mannered, and clearly envious man who appeared intent on silencing someone more brash and outwardly flamboyant. And he proposed using medication to silence me. Needless to say, I emphatically disagreed with his

DIAGRAM 1

Address	Dates	Rent	Living Accomodations	Health Insurance	Employer	Position	FT/PT Temp	Reason for leaving
1) Far Northwest	11/90-2/91	NO	couch	NO	grocery store	bagger	PT	
2) Melrose	2/91*-6/91	YES	sleeping room	NO	grocery store	bagger	PT	terminated

*2/91 - hospitalized 21 days (NMH-Lawson YMCA) for bipolar disorder/depression

Address	Dates	Rent	Living Accomodations	Health Insurance	Employer	Position	FT/PT Temp	Reason for leaving
3) Delaware	6/91-9/91	YES	shared studio	NO	unemployed/restaurant	unemployed/waiter	PT	
4) Division	9/91-11/92	YES	couch	NO	restaurant	waiter	PT	terminated
5) Hoyne	11/92-...	NO	bedroom	NO	unemployed/	unemployed/	PT	
6) Hermitage	–	YES	floor	NO	restaurant	waiter	PT	
7) Division	–	YES	couch	NO	restaurant	waiter	PT	
8) Hoyne	...-4/93	NO	bedroom	NO	restaurant/unemployed	waiter/unemployed	PT	terminated
9) San Diego, California	4/93-7/94	YES	bedroom	NO	unemployed/financial temp.	unemployed/financial temp.	temp	
10) Irving Park	7/94-8/97	YES	bedroom	NO	financial temp	financial temp	temp	
11) Bittersweet	9/97-present	YES	bedroom	NO**	financial temp/treatment center/unemployed	financial temp/therapist/unemployed	temp/FT	temp/terminated

**Health insurance from 5/00 to 3/01

academic understanding of mania, linking it to depression and speaking of it as being the other side of the same pathological coin.

> "No way, Doc. That which you call mania is what I call normal. All I need you to do is help me return to normal and I'll be on my way."

Unbeknownst to me, my family back in California had done a little investigating of its own. Based on only a handful of breathlessly rambling and excruciatingly monotonous phone calls they'd received from me over the preceding months, they had concluded that I was suffering from bipolar disorder. Also at about this time, my girlfriend and I had broken up and I had found a sleeping room in a festive Chicago neighborhood known as "Boystown" (Melrose, Diagram 1). Though earning minimum wage at the grocery store, I was able to meet the requirement for rent ($125/month) for a few months, anyway.

Refusing medication, I was hospitalized for depression in February 1991. This is peak season for the mental health industry, so beds were at a premium. As a result, I agreed to stay at the hospital's emergency overflow unit located on the fifth floor of the Lawson YMCA. The emergency unit treated acute cases of mental illness, like mine, and was operated and staffed by Northwestern Memorial Hospital. Much to my delight, I fit right in. And right on cue, I returned to "normal" within 10 days. Diagnoses meant absolutely nothing to me. At this point, only two characteristics about my condition were clear to me: depression is bad and stick me in a room full of non-threatening people and my depression lifts almost immediately.

I recall that a couple people who appeared very similar to me were called schizophrenic. I also recall flirting with one of them, a young black woman, every evening. I would tell her boundless stories about the dance clubs I would frequent. I also recall one woman who was very odd. She was about 45, but spoke like an 8 year-old child, with physical features to match. There was a gay couple, the elder of the two was a theatrical, middle-aged man who worked as a travel agent. Nothing about him seemed abnormal; he was struggling with a bout of major depression. The younger man, about forty, was a quiet, modest schizophrenic dying of AIDS. I recall him sharing his peculiar stories with me. I got the impression that he was both proud and ashamed of his unusual musings. I, however, was enchanted by them and made comparisons to Gabriel Garcia Marquez' *One Hundred Years of Solitude.* I loaned him my cherished copy of the book and mentioned that many consider Marquez a genius. I encouraged him to write his thoughts down. I even brought him to my apartment after I was released from the hospital so that he could save his stories on my computer.

Another depressed, middle-aged, gay man couldn't get enough of me, my neon clothes, and my flamboyant nature. He was an artist and he took pleasure in making me the centerpiece of his work. His masterpiece was affectionately entitled "Neon Psycho Warrior." Upon learning that I was a recovering alcoholic, he decided that he was one, too. And with that he asked me to sponsor him. *Why not?* This union was short lived, however. I fired him a couple of weeks later for standing me up after I hadn't returned one of his phone calls.

Then there was Darto, a young Brazilian man in his early twenties. He didn't talk much – more precisely, he couldn't talk much, as his jaw was wired shut. In fact, everything on his entire body that could be wired shut, was. Only several weeks before, Darto had thrown back a bottle of whiskey before throwing himself out of his apartment window. He lived on the fourteenth floor of a Chicago high rise.

As some had taken a special interest in me, I was mesmerized by this unsuspecting miracle whom I called Darto. It was clear from his poor English and thick accent that Darto hadn't been in the states long. With much labor, he explained that he had come to the states, in part to go to college, and in part to escape his family. He indicated that his family expected him to take over the family business, of which he wanted no part. Apparently, he attended a school in one of the Dakotas because they had established an exchange program with Brazilian students.

Upon completing his college education, Darto found himself at a crossroads. He had to go somewhere, but he refused to return home to his family. So one day, he grabbed a bottle of whiskey and a dart, and threw back a few stiff shots, then tossed the dart at a map of the United States. The dart landed next to Chicago. Ergo, this is how he both wound up in Chicago and received the moniker, Darto, Portuguese for "dart." I did my best to make him laugh despite himself. I got the impression that he appreciated my efforts to do so.

If you are familiar with the Burt Reynolds film, "Deliverance," you're likely familiar with the reference to "Dueling Banjoes." For the rest of you, the reference is used to conjure up the disturbing image of a soulless, toothless, banjo-playing hillbilly boy. The troublesome story to follow is only a slight variation on "Dueling Banjoes." I call it "Dueling Bipolars."

Lastly, there was the Captain, a diminutive, 56 year-old bipolar, who, incidentally, was recovering from open-heart surgery. The Captain worked as a freelancer in advertising, and his resume appeared complete. It included both Wacker Drive in Chicago and Madison Avenue in New York City. Moreover, the Captain had big plans for the future, and I was all ears.

The Captain had decided that he was going to develop a non-petroleum based economy. *Of course!* Having grown up in a scenic, coastal, northern California town, I applauded the work of activists, like my parents, who fought to keep offshore oilrigs out of our sacred waters. *Oil is the root of all evil, both home and abroad!* I sat with the Captain each night, and together we breathed life into his ideas.

Hydrogen is the solution and solar fission is the means. Ideally, all buildings should be pyramidal in shape, to maximize their exposure to sunlight. Cities like Chicago are ideal for this plan, as it has both a convenient and abundant water supply.

Oh yeah, man, this is big! I decided that what we needed most at this point (aside from medication) was credibility. So I committed the services of my professor of economics back home in California. At my urging and dogged efforts as a research assistant, he had recently published an article through the Oxford University Press. In fact, I knew that he happened to be writing an economics textbook at the time. I also knew that he had received his Ph.D. in agricultural economics and that he was ecologically sound. *He'd do it! He'd write an abstract for our paper and put his name on it.* I confirmed that my professor was onboard via a 6:00 a.m. wake-up call – that's Central Time. I woke him from a dead sleep, raving incoherently about his role in our grand scheme. "A brief mission statement is already in the mail," I exclaimed. Poor professor.

The mission statement that I had promised was a document no more than 100 words in length that I had written in my wildest of minds. I was exceedingly delighted by the volumes of information that I had managed to transcribe in those 100 words. I had read it over-and-over, time-and-time again – *it was a compelling piece of work, indeed!* Years later and just prior to destroying it, I read it one last time. Oddly, this reading brought to my attention for the first time a most curious phrase, from an even more curious document. In my attempt to describe myself as an expert, having studied many *disciplines*, what I wrote instead, and incidentally took to the world having used this statement as a business card, was that I had studied with many *disciples*. (I'm guessing about twelve of them.)

Besides our plans to change the world, the Captain and I decided to get an apartment together (Delaware, Diagram 1). This seemed to be in the best interests of our mission. Still refusing medication, I had broken through my listlessness with a brilliance that I feared would never return. *Thank God I'm normal again!* In fact, while most of the patients were remaining on the unit indefinitely, I was told that I was being discharged after just ten days. Things were only just starting to improve, however, so I pleaded with my doctor and the mental health staff to allow me to stay longer. "These people are like family to me. They are all I have. And I feel so much better about myself. This has helped me so much. Can't I stay a little longer?" My doctor understood all of this to be true. He understood that I was alone, mentally ill, and refusing medication. He understood that I was two thousand miles from home and months, perhaps years, from reconciling with my family of origin.

I would have remained on the unit indefinitely had it not been for the Viet Nam "assassin" that had been assigned as my roommate. He was 6'4"and 250 pounds of unadulterated rage. He hated everyone, had a vendetta against his ex-wife, his employer (whom he had held out of a window), the U.S. government, and on-and-on. He made everyone on the floor, including staff, feel incredibly uncomfortable in his presence. Needless to say, I said my good-byes after just two days with him. In all, I stayed on the unit for 21 days. I returned to Melrose as delighted and hopeful as ever. Naturally, my doctor was concerned and continued to urge me to take medication. This only triggered the by now tiresome rebuttal:

> "Doc, this is 'normal.' I'm used to feeling this way. I'm not used to feeling listless. I agree that you've helped me get past that. But don't tell me that you don't want me to feel the way I feel. Don't tell me that there is something wrong with me. This is me. This is normal. Besides, you originally recommended that I go on an antidepressant, but the fog has lifted without medication."

Note, "normal" here; i.e., in the working model, is equivalent to hopelessly manic.

Mania is a wonderfully irreverent and invincible experience of unfounded elation accompanied by hyperactivity, talkativeness, and impractical, grandiose plans. To the mentally ill, it is unrealized fortune and fame already internalized. To the mental health professional, it is potentially destructive and requires medication maintenance and possibly hospitalization. Onset typically occurs in one's twenties and childhood depression is not a predictor of bipolar disorder. In my case, a manic episode typically lasts longer than six months, running from early-May to mid-October. Each end of a manic cycle is likely to include a less than full-blown state of mania called hypomania. Consequently, I appeared manic for up to (the same) nine months of a year. For these reasons, manic was my desired, if not normal, state. It is worth noting that, in most cases, any attempt to curb or treat a manic episode is met with fierce resistance, anger, and even rage.

This digression about mania is leading to something – unemployment. Once again, I had metamorphosed from stoic recluse back to incessant chatterbox. And my employer, the grocery store, took note of my transformation and began to watch me very closely.

As far as I was concerned, this job was the closest I had ever come to the military. Corporals hovered over the rank and file with a watchful eye. Too much talking was grounds for discipline. Corporals then reported back to sergeants about the logistics of their covert mission: Operation Hush. There was no secret about it. I was in the crosshairs for repeated acts of irreverence and insubordination. *They want to watch me? I'll give them something to watch.* And the rank and file and I will have a good laugh about it, later.

Ultimately, I was called into my supervisor's office. The objective at this point was to scare me straight. My supervisor started in on me, recounting numerous acts of insubordination. Insubordination was their favorite word. *Insubordination? I bag groceries, for Christ's sake! Nothing I do here could ever warrant the use of the term "insubordination."* When she was finished rambling about insubordination, it was my turn to unleash a stinging assault of my own. I told this woman, in no uncertain terms, that she was:

> "... the most pathetic excuse for a human being I had ever met. You are cold, rigid, and painfully unfriendly. You must hate yourself – everyone else does. You act like this is the military with your 'insubordination.' It's a grocery store! You look down on (the rank and file) as if you've attained some position of status, yet your job appears to be nothing more than babysitting me."

This woman took herself far too seriously not to cry when I left her office.

When I showed up for my next shift, the corporal advised me that the sergeant wanted to see me in his barracks. I knew then that the party was over. "If he's got something to say to me, tell him to say it to me right here." "Right here," meaning in front of the customers and, more importantly, the rank and file. Within minutes, the sergeant emerged from his barracks and proceeded to terminate me. But as soon as he made that point crystal clear, I took off my apron and, rather than handing it to him, tossed it in his face... yes, for the world to see. That's another seldom talked about symptom of a manic episode – if you're going to go, go out in style.

When floridly manic, unemployment feels just like sweet freedom and a million dollars in the bank! Within a month, I had lost my girlfriend, lost my job, and lost my grip on reality. Sadly, this pattern of loss has remained a dominant one in my life. One might suspect that the cumulative impact of losses I had incurred over the previous two years alone might throw one prone to depression into a woeful state:

1) I had given up alcohol.
2) I had dropped out of graduate school and had seemingly walked away from a promising future as an economist.
3) After migrating to the Midwest, I had alienated my family and friends back home.
4) I then alienated myself from my dear friends in Champaign.
5) Ultimately, I alienated myself from Alcoholics Anonymous.
6) At this point, other than my doctor, the Captain is the only person I'd maintained contact with for more than a month.
7) Two relationships had failed.
8) I had lost my employability, taking a remedial, minimum wage job that I couldn't keep.
9) I had briefly lost touch with reality.
10) I had come to learn that I was mentally ill.

Sure, I've got cause for depression. In fact, I've got to believe that the reasonable man would be incredibly depressed if his can't-miss life had taken the nosedive mine had. But therein lies the omnipotence of mania. My life, as far as I could discern, was right on track. Only that track included one modest feat, that of developing a non-petroleum based economy powered by hydrogen via solar fission.

Although I continued to see my doctor three days a week, his tone was beginning to change, as was mine. He informed me that he would like to see me indefinitely. Unfortunately, the business office had instructed him that, unless I made some good faith effort to pay for my hospitalization and weekly sessions, my services would be discontinued.

"You've got to be kidding? I have no health insurance and I have no income. Besides, I feel a lot better than I did a few months ago. I really don't see the need for continuing."

Eventually, my doctor was forced to terminate my treatment. As he did, he shared these parting remarks:

If you feel the need to contact me in the future, please do so. I will continue to see you. All the business office requires is that you contact them to make arrangements for payment. They are simply interested in you working with them in good faith.

For a couple of extremely focused weeks that summer, I poured all of my energy (about equal to that of twelve disciples, I suppose) into research on hydrogen as a viable fuel alternative. The fact that I was not a physicist was not relevant. I was something better (manic) — *a metaphysicist, you know, like Jesus.* As disturbing as all of this sounds, consider this: I would head out each night by myself and end up at the end of the evening with the young woman of my choosing. I demonstrated this feat time-and-time again, often to the amazement of those around me. Dance clubs are a wonderful playground for the floridly manic. The loud music, the flashing strobe and bright neon lights, the disco ball orbiting high above, and all of the beautiful people acting normal for a change. Indeed, in small doses, mania can be a seductive experience to all.

In the meantime, the Captain and I grew increasingly intolerant of one another. For whatever reason, he had been taking his medication, lithium — the same medication I refused.

Before too long, he was far less urgent about our endeavor and much more practical, overall. *That's really starting to piss me off!* Worse yet, he started calling me "impossible" and "manic." He even went as far as to insist that I find a job and start taking medication. *BETRAYED! You sell out! You little bastard!* Such accusations were fighting words, and, considering the Captain's post-operative health, they led to a near tragic altercation. In the end, we both agreed that I was too big for our little domicile, and that I had to go.

By the time I bid the Captain, and my manifest destiny as savior, adieu, I could sense the brightness beginning to recede. Fearful of another listless interlude of stoic isolation, I decided to find work as a waiter. Although my social skills are both dazzling and at times mesmerizing when manic (most of the year), by contrast, when depressed I am severely retarded socially. So, in a moment of unequalled clarity, I chose a line of work that would force me to engage with people while I struggled with a bout of depression. Fortunately, I got hired right away at, of all places for a so-called recovering alcoholic, a bar dressed up as a restaurant.

THE LOOKOUTS
Chapter 2
JEFF'S WATCH

By September 1991, the looming darkness was slowly taking over. *Son-of-a bitch! My doctor said this would happen.* Suddenly, I was painfully aware of my summer long intoxication with the Captain's grandiose plans. *What a jackass (I am)! Never again!* And with that, I found myself giving my doctor a call.

> "I'm starting to lose it, again, just like you said. Can I come back? I have a job, now. I'll call the business office to make arrangements for payment. I've seen enough, Doc. I'm ready to begin taking medication."

I resumed seeing my doctor immediately.

My doctor was not bipolar. He was as steady as I was turbulent. With few exceptions – most notably, my decision to call the business office, to return to treatment, and to begin taking medication – nothing that I did or said ever shocked, delighted, encouraged, or disappointed him. For someone like me who was bent on entertaining others, he truly was a tough crowd.

> I'm going to start you on an antidepressant and 900 mg of lithium carbonate. Lithium is an elemental salt that acts as a mood stabilizer. Since lithium affects the level of serotonin, a neurotransmitter in the brain, it is hypothesized that bipolar disorder is caused by aberrant brain chemistry. To oversimplify, it's like saying that your brain's secretion of salt is irregular. 900 mg is a rather small dose of lithium; you likely will experience only mild tremors, increased thirst, and more frequent urination. You won't be on the antidepressant long. I just want to bring your mood up to a level at which I can stabilize you.

Shortly after, while at the restaurant, I met those who would emerge as the most important actors in my life to this day, some ten years later. Jeff, a gay waiter who happens to be something of a caretaker, took an immediate interest in my sad case and encouraged me to discuss my predicament with him.

"I am being forced to move and have no place to go. I'm considering returning to San Francisco. I'm an alcoholic, and I just learned that I'm bipolar. They tell me it used to be called manic-depression. Anyway, I've just been put on medication because I'm starting a cycle of depression, which is why I seem the way I do."

Fortunately, Jeff, like the rest of the planet, I presume, was as oblivious to bipolar disorder as I. Without consulting his roommate, Nancy, he discouraged me from returning to California and offered me his couch, instead. *Really? I would love to stay in Chicago!* And this was how "Jeff's watch" began. Interestingly, Jeff had a voracious appetite for alcohol. Neither this, nor our differences in sexuality, complicated our peculiar, yet priceless, relationship.

This placed me at Division (Diagram 1) in September 1991. The thirteen months I lived with Jeff and Nancy were marked by unparalleled stability. Of course, stability is a relative term. And trying to measure a period of stability in my life is tantamount to trying to observe peace in the Middle East. As I was battling against depression and the accompanying compulsion to both isolate and alienate myself from the rest of the world, Jeff helped me integrate with the other waitstaff. This was relatively easy, as Jeff was immensely popular with everyone from dishwasher and busboy, to manager, to waitress, queen and jock, alike. Moreover, he was on the fast track to becoming the schedule writer, the most powerful duty assigned the waitstaff. If it weren't for this very fact, I never would have lasted at the restaurant those thirteen months.

For all intents and purposes, being assigned schedule writer meant one thing: Jeff gave his friends preferential treatment.

> What days do you want off? What section do you want
> to work in? How many tables do you want? What time
> do you want to leave? Who do you want to work with?

And to make life interesting, for every waiter or waitress Jeff called friend, he despised two more. If nothing else, it was politically shrewd to gain Jeff's approval. Needless to say, when Jeff introduced me to the others as his new roommate, I was not only assumed to be gay but, more importantly, both readily accepted and instantly popular, as well.

Jeff introduced me to Keith, Todd, and the jocks, the queens, the bartenders, and Michelle and the waitresses. Amazingly, ten years have passed and I continue to see Jeff and Keith regularly and to talk to Michelle, who now lives in New York City, at least once a month.

I soon discovered that I had a lot in common with a lot of people. A waiter told me that he suffered from major depression and a waitress shared that she is a recovering alcoholic, too. But none had as much in common with me as Jeff. Like myself, Jeff is a rabid sports fan. In addition to our interest in sports, he and I shared a passion for dancing – not real popular among straight, overly self-conscience, single white males. Consequently, Jeff and I were inseparable for those thirteen months. Our daily routine was this simple:

> wake up 2:30 p.m. and get dressed
> lunch 3:00 p.m. with friends at the restaurant

> work   4:00 p.m. until 2:00 a.m.
> hang out at a nearby bar   2:30 a.m. until 5:00 a.m.
> shower   5:15 a.m.
> sleep   5:30 a.m. until 2:30 p.m.

One of the many perks that went with schedule writing was that Jeff was able to assign his closest friends the same days off so that we were able to enjoy our leisure time together. Consequently, we spent our summer days playing tennis or sunbathing in the bleachers of historic Wrigley Field. But during the evening hours, Jeff and I headed for the nightclubs. I can remember dancing frenetically and tirelessly, without interruption, for more than three full hours each night.

By May 1992, I was feeling my old self; i.e., "normal," once again. This is a curious statement for many reasons, most notably, because I had been mistaking the energy level of adult mania with the energy exerted throughout my childhood, adolescence, and early adult years in response to depression. In other words, I had always seen myself as having worked diligently. Therefore, the hyperactivity that accompanied mania was interpreted as representative of the work ethic and energy that I had long displayed.

Consequently, I considered mania normal. By contrast, the cataleptic depression that I had recently experienced seemed like an altogether new phenomenon.

Also by this time, I had established a core group of friends. Equally important, no fewer than twenty other acquaintances could say that they had known me the past nine months.

> "Thanks again, Doc, but no thanks. I feel fine and my life seems to be back on track. I guess I don't need your help or this lithium any more."

As irresponsible and negligent as this sounds, keep in mind, I'd only begun to formulate an understanding of this condition called bipolar disorder. At that point, my return to sound body and mind left me with the illusion that my condition was curable, or more precisely, that it had been cured. In the meantime, I had been constructing my own working model of bipolar disorder, and found myself pondering this dilemma:

> *Not only do I like myself and others when I'm feeling normal, others like me, too. So why on earth would I*

want to tamper with my mood at a time like this? No medication. Double down on mania and let it ride!

In time, I would learn like most others, the hard way.

By early spring 1992, I pursued Michelle relentlessly and eventually wore her down. Though not terribly charming, this technique has proved reliable over the years. For the next five-and-a-half years, Michelle, Jeff, and ultimately medication, combined as my life's stabilizing force. Again, one is confronted with the task of measuring stability. Borrowing from seismology, compare an acute tremor that measures 3.4 on the Richter scale to a quake that measures 6.9. Neither event is considered desirable, yet the former could be described as being more stable than the latter.

By fall 1992, mania was beginning to recede, though I clearly remained hypomanic. Shortly thereafter, irritability and restlessness began to disrupt my charmed life. The first sign was my unfounded attack on Nancy during a discussion about renewing the apartment lease. To make a regrettable story short, I argued fiercely with Jeff to exclude Nancy from the new lease. Tragically, anger, ruthlessness, and lack of compassion for others accompany profound mood swings, leaving a path of destruction in their wake. Poor Jeff and Nancy. Sensing that I was growing increasingly surly, Jeff had asked Keith and others to keep an eye on me while he was out of town for two days. To this day, both take full responsibility for my firing. Poor Jeff and Keith.

Jeff had specifically assigned Keith to a section next to me so as to keep me happy and out of trouble. Keith and I recall the events of that evening vividly. He and I were upstairs in the smoking section and a "12-top" of Iowa football fans was carrying on during an Iowa-NC State college football game. To liven things up a bit, Keith and I ran past the Iowa table waving red (NC State color) towels every time NC State scored. By design, this drew the ire of the Iowa fans. This was all done in good fun. After all, we did want them to tip us at the end of the night.

Then, some Southern, aristocrat-wanna-be and his companion sat down in my station and ordered a scotch, a couple of burgers, and onion rings. After his food arrived, he waved me down and requested a new basket of onion rings. No big deal – they're just onion rings. "I'll get you a fresh basket." This kind of thing happens all of the time. What was to follow does not.

When I returned with his onion rings, he accused me of having mistaken him for someone that I could have intentionally dumped this "shit" (the onion rings) on. It was hard to take someone in that restaurant, who took himself so seriously, very serious. Baffled, and not knowing whether Don Quixote was actually serious or merely seriously delusional, I chuckled and pointed out that I had, in fact, replaced the first basket of onion rings with a fresh basket. This only made him more indignant, and he barked his accusation at me a second time. *This prick is pissed at me!* Lookout!

All of the safeguards in the world couldn't save me now. I leaned across his table and got within inches of his haggard face and requested that he repeat those words one more time. He did. So I stood up and with great irreverence said, "So, there's something wrong with your food. Let me take care of that for you." As the legend has it, with a bear-like swat I snatched every morsel of food, burger-and-all, from Don Quixote's plate, walked over to the bus stand, and tossed his dinner into the garbage. I then walked down to the bar, pulled up a seat, and announced to the bartender, "I just got fired!"

Only now, ten years later, I'm beginning to see hypomania as a dangerous state. Of course, when it comes to bipolar disorder, that's not saying a whole lot. The difficulty with hypomania, however, is that the restlessness, irritability, and rage of depression accompany the manic behavior. By contrast, pure, unadulterated mania is characterized by boundless energy and pleasure seeking. Just as sleep gets squeezed out, so to do bad feelings. Nothing and nobody can upset the manic. Those who should try only fail miserably and look comical in the process, which, in turn, merely heightens the manic's delight. Despite the effort of others, this entire process is orchestrated by the manic every step of the way.

Anyway, those days remain the most carefree and happiest of my life. For the first time since early childhood, I didn't feel as though being flawed was at all life threatening. For the first time in my adulthood, I didn't feel as though I were falling behind and that I would never realize my full potential or live up to some unapproachable standard or lofty expectation of myself that I

47

had usurped from someone, somewhere, likely as early as child-hood. I was on sabbatical! A good case could be made for the argument that this sabbatical remains a work in progress today, some ten years later.

Within the past year I have recounted my childhood in psy-chotherapy, and this has helped me to recognize that I've been dealing with depression since an early age. To combat, or more precisely, to cope with excruciating boredom, mur-derous resentment, and general dislike of everyone (including family) and everything around me – interestingly, the same phenomenon I now call depression – I turned, not to drugs, but to my own physical and mental gifts and capacities.

I have always said that the voice of my internal monologue bellowed from a football coach:

> *110% – that's what it's going to take! Come on! What's the matter with you? Are you just going to lay down and die? Life is full of adversity. You need to kick adversity right in the ass! Fatigue makes cowards of us all! You'll never reach your full potential unless you give it every-thing you've got, every time! There are no timeouts in life!*

My guess is that for me, like my grandfather, football was my first love. However, I wasn't allowed to play organized football until I was fourteen. So I imagined what it must take to become a football player. The internal monologue recited above is what I conjured up. (Careful not to fall into the trap that this whole discussion has anything to do with football or football coaches, or my parents not allowing me to play organized football until I was fourteen.) This is a discussion about coping with childhood depression.

Of course I was terrified of not keeping up, of being called lethargic, or of being accused of being tired or fatigued, or of not giving it my all:

Something's wrong with me. And this is something I guard hypervigilantly. To be safe, I disguise it through a tireless work ethic and over-achievement, so that no one will suspect. But when no one is watching, and I'm not required to perform, I'm overcome by relentless self-loathing and the dreadful wish to blowup my hometown and everyone in it, namely me.

Apparently, others feel the same way I do. Consider both the high school gunmen and the lyrics of English pop star Morrissey.

Appropriately, from the album "Viva Hate," Morrissey's disenchantment with the small, coastal town in "Everyday is Like Sunday" rings eerily true of my contempt for the tiny, excruciatingly boring, fog covered, seafaring town in which I was raised. In this very popular song the artist describes himself in his solitude, longing for the immediate annihilation of this gray, seaside town.

Tragically, this was the way I approached my entire life. A secretive, depressed child imagining what it must take to be... a graduate student (insert some unapproachable standard and lofty expectations here) and wondering how on earth I was going to pull it off. Worse yet, what would happen if someone finally unmasked me in the meantime only to discover that they had made a horrible mistake by admitting me to their program and awarding me a fellowship? Ever since childhood, *I'm better off dead* was always the most accessible solution.

Why, then, was I resigned to suffer in silence? Many forces conspired against me from an early age. Two of which are our cultural naiveté and denial of mental illness. In short, our nation's denial of mental illness not only reinforces our dearth of knowledge and information about the subject, but it stigmatizes and isolates the mentally ill in the process. Ultimately, the mentally ill feel trapped:

I'm going to make a lot of good people – people that I and others look up to, people who point to me as a role model for others – look really stupid if I open my mouth.

In other words, there is a powerful catch-22 in place. Hard work to escape depression is rewarded by recognition, which, in turn, reinforces the hard work and intensifies the need to conceal one's flaws. Isolation, then, can be understood as an adaptive response that attempts to conceal one's flaws.

For those prone to fits of denial, I would like to say that it really was that bad all of those years. To my credit, I merely convinced everyone around me that it wasn't. At an early age, I had discerned what are and are not acceptable feelings and behavior. My irritability, restlessness, self-loathing, and hatred of everyone – especially family – and everything around me clearly are among those feelings deemed not acceptable.

It might seem peculiar that upon receiving a fellowship to graduate school and seemingly having the world on a string, my efforts to kill myself, then ultimately to disappear, escalated. Within days of receiving notice of the fellowship award, I was handing twelve thousand dollars to a church pitchman with designs on fleeing the country, like some war criminal. That alone says a lot about how bad it really was. It really was really bad for a really long time. My desire to die was recurrent. My attempt to disappear, then, can be understood as a response to a lifelong war against depression; one that I was losing miserably by seemingly winning – my star glimmered brightly from a relatively young age. The irony is that had I done something less exemplary, like attempted suicide or hurt a classmate, I would have received treatment at an earlier age.

Since the time of the fellowship award, I have witnessed my own rapid demise into a pauper-like state of relative unemployability. All the more reason for one with a lifelong penchant to die to be so inclined. And yet, since taking lithium in relatively small doses, I've not once considered suicide a solution. It cannot be denied that these are rather compelling arguments.

With very few exceptions, all of which can be found in the writings of the "great (dead) authors," the only words I found solace in were those penned by my contemporary, Morrissey. The fact that Morrissey was discussing forbidden love in "The Boy with the Thorn in His Side" never kept me from adopting it as my anthem during my college years. The artist describes the murderous hatred that boils over from the intolerable position of being misunderstood, or worse, not taken seriously. The outcome, once again, is angst filled alienation.

Unemployed, unmedicated, and losing my manic edge, I went searching for restaurant work. As restaurants go, fall is a difficult time of the year in Chicago. Things naturally slow down after Labor Day and waitstaffs get trimmed. Besides,

I wasn't exactly feeling as dazzling as I once had. As the job search continued without any success, I began to feel like a burden to Jeff and Nancy. Over their objections, I moved in with Michelle and her roommate. That put me at Hoyne in November 1992.

Fortunately, the same chain that had terminated me in September rehired me at their new location. The managers at the previous store had explained that they hated to see me go, but given the circumstances, their hands were tied. It was now late November and I had somehow evaded a full-blown attack of depression. Instead, I remained hypomanic and both extremely vulnerable yet highly invulnerable, seemingly carefree yet increasingly harsh and critical toward some, most notably, toward Michelle's roommate, with whom I was now living rent-free. As with Nancy, in my turbulent, hypomanic state, I found the audacity to make this young woman feel like the third wheel in her own apartment.

"What's her problem? Does she have something to say to me? Tell her I said she can go to hell." Poor woman.

For any number of good reasons, Michelle and I split up before too long. Having seen this coming, I informed everyone at work that I might need a place to live for a little while. I didn't call Jeff (right away), because he worked closely and remained good friends with Michelle. At the time, I believed Michelle and I needed some distance from each other. A waitress I had been chumming around with offered me some space in her apartment; she and her boyfriend shared a one-bedroom garden apartment. "Sounds good, what's my rent? $75 a month, great! I was hoping for under $100." That placed me at Hermitage.

To most observers, I was sleeping on a hardwood floor surrounded by my life's belongings and separated from the rest of the apartment by a thin, plastic shower curtain. To my bedazzled eyes, however, I had been given the key to a penthouse at the Ritz-Carlton. Interestingly, some theorists maintain that mania is analogous to a well-known defense mechanism, denial, in that the individual unconsciously distorts reality so as to protect against anxiety, confrontation, depression, and the like. Here (and elsewhere, for that matter), this explanation seems to fit.

My new roommates could only take so much of me, however. After just one month they politely asked me to leave. At this point, I had no choice but to give Jeff a call, something that I was reluctant to do because of his close relationship with Michelle. In the end, however, I gave him a ring. That conversation went something like this:

> Marc: Hey, it's me.
> Jeff: What's up, buddy?
> Marc: They said I can't stay here any more.
> Jeff: You want to pack your things and I'll come get you?
> Marc: Yeah.
> Jeff: I'll be there in fifteen minutes.

This returned me to the couch at Division Street by mid-January 1993, and, by Cupid's design, right back in the company of Michelle. Sure enough, our worst fears were realized almost immediately when we both expressed how much we missed each other. We resumed dating and within a little more than a month, I had returned to Michelle, her roommate, and their apartment on Hoyne. And thus began "Michelle's watch."

Disclaimer: "Viva Hate" was released in 1988, nearly four years after I had moved away to college and several years since these morose sentiments first surfaced in me. Any comparisons are strictly coincidental.

Chapter 3
MICHELLE'S WATCH

Meanwhile, I continued to discount what my doctor had told me about mania, linking it to depression and referring to it as the other side of the same pathological coin.

That's bookish. Purely theoretical interpretation on his part. Evidence, however, suggests quite the opposite: I am more likable manic.

Incredibly, despite my experience over the previous summer, I remained convinced that mania was simply getting a bad rap.

Hypomania returned, but this time the depression was lurking. To my disbelief, however, Michelle was relieved. She told me that she actually liked me better when I was feeling depressed than when I was manic.

> You are dizzying and annoying to be around, even to listen to. Sometimes, I'm afraid of what's going to come out of your mouth next. But when you're feeling depressed, you're much more real and easy to follow.

Before long, I grew intolerably irritable, restless, and critical of others and things around me. For various reasons, Michelle shared my discontent. So we decided that, since we were working in restaurants, we might as well do so in a resort-like setting. At the time, San Diego satisfied a lot of our criteria: warm climate, picturesque, miles of beach, oceanfront living, oceanfront restaurants, large population, and hundreds of miles from family. Converting distance on the West Coast to a scale used by the rest of the country, San Diego is roughly three or four states south of San Francisco.

By this time, I had reconciled with my parents. They began sharing with me what it was like to be my parents two thousand miles away. They told me that they had done some investigating and had concluded that I was bipolar. They had begun attending a support group for family members of bipolars only to learn this harsh reality:

> Not only is there nothing you can do for your family member, but the more pressure you apply, the more the individual will resist and pull away.

It thus became my father's job to police my mother, who was determined to fly to Chicago and rescue me. Poor mom and dad. Fortunately, this dialogue made laughter possible once again. My parents would recount some of the most exhilarating yet inane, both breathless and breathe-taking stories from Chicago. As neither had the opportunity to speak, each admitted to being exhausted just listening.

Unfortunately, each time I visit my family, even today, I become painfully aware of things about them, about my sleepy hometown, and about the San Francisco Bay Area that trigger my irritability, restlessness, and harsh criticism. Not coincidentally, these pilgrimages home occur over the holidays, or, more specifically, during those months concurring with depression.

With hypomania, irritability, restlessness, and harsh criticism are readily accessible. Before Michelle and I could leave for San Diego, I had time to squeeze in another firing and another month of unemployment in Chicago. It was early March 1993 and I was working a lunch shift at the restaurant. On that day, the kitchen, which had a history of running long ticket times, was running excessively long ticket times. To me, however, they were:

> ...*functioning intolerably slow and completely incompetent! This is bullshit! And they (the kitchen workers, who are hourly labor) couldn't care less. This doesn't affect them, but it sure as hell is coming out of my pocket!*

Customers were notorious for taking anything and everything out on the waitstaff in the form of diminishing tips. So I stormed back to the kitchen and "threw some gasoline on the fire."

"What the fuck's the problem back here? You realize that I consistently have 60 minute ticket times?
You realize that when people don't get their food
timely, or are late to work because of you idiots, I
can't make any money? Come on, Ced (a very large
and now enraged head cook), say something! This in
on you, pal. Don't just stand there like an idiot!"

That was about the time a couple of things occurred. First,
Ced made a move toward me (others intervened), explaining what he was about to do to my lily-white ass. Then, my
manager, who had been within earshot of my entire tirade,
emerged from his office and quickly removed me from the
kitchen. Since he knew my history and had heard the entire
exchange, the rest was mere formality. He handed me my
termination papers and bid me farewell.

*Farewell, Chicago, indeed. It's been real, but I can't leave you
fast enough!* To help finance our move, Michelle sold her
car. Poor Michelle. We arrived in San Diego in April of
1993, a day or two ahead of schedule. This was significant
because upon arrival, we were without jobs, without a car,

without an apartment, and forced to live out of a Ryder truck, which, incidentally, had to be returned by the week's end.

Fortunately, we found a little beach bungalow located on a strip of sand nestled between two bodies of water, Mission Bay and the Pacific Ocean. We next bought the first car off of the first lot we found. And Michelle, who is as likeable and playful as she is strikingly attractive, at nearly six feet tall and barely 130 pounds, found work waiting tables immediately in nearby affluent La Jolla. We were amazed to discover that Michelle's tips often exceeded 40 percent and, on occasion, reached 100 percent. In fact, Michelle was beside herself on the rare instance that a tip was only 20 percent. She would complain to me about it for a while, then we would laugh at our friends back in Chicago, who had to put up with that lousy weather, that lousy restaurant, and, most of all, its lousy tipping clientele.

Meanwhile, I couldn't find work and so my unemployment dragged on for more than a month. Like Jeff, Michelle was less critical and more tolerant of me than I was of others. With depression setting in, however, my unemployment started eating at me. Typical of depression, enjoyable experiences lost their pleasure; even the lure of the beach had already worn thin. And San Diegans seemed more like aliens than fellow Californians. Compared to Chicago, San Diego was subdued and its citizenry seemed overcome by apathy. Of course, such harsh criticism was never too far away when my mood was headed south.

Fearful that depression was imminent, I scheduled an appointment with a psychiatrist through the community mental health center, right away. My greatest motivator was the fear that I had dragged Michelle out to California only to put her through an episode of cataleptic depression. To put it frankly, the psychiatrist was aghast with me:

> You just picked up and moved to San Diego, and now you don't have a job? What are you going to do for money? San Diego is in the midst of a major recession. You mean to tell me you are bipolar and that you stopped taking your medication? Do you realize that you have a chronic, progressive condition? Do you realize how dangerous it is to go off your medication? How many times have you been

on lithium? Twice! Did you know that each time you go off an effective medication, it loses some of its effectiveness? Did you know that? At this stage, I'm not certain that lithium will continue to be effective, Mr. Pollard. What do you think about that?

I was horrified. I was more fearful for Michelle than for myself for she had sacrificed so much for us. She had been supporting me for more than two months, had defended me to her friends and family time-and-time again, and had sold her car to finance our move. My negligence now jeopardized everything, but worse yet, threatened to tarnish her once brilliant future. Due to a scheduling conflict, that was the only time I met with that particular psychiatrist. But since that memorable day in the spring of 1993, I have not once considered discontinuing my lithium treatment.

I returned to lithium for good and finally began working as a financial temporary. Meanwhile, Michelle decided to enroll in a graduate program at the University of San Diego, in addition to waitressing part-time. U.S.D. happens to be one of the more expensive universities in the country. Consequently, Michelle borrowed twelve thousand dollars for her nine-month program. Between my medication maintenance, her student loan and tips, and the peanut shells I started bringing home, things slowly began to improve.

San Diego is not much of a city, as far as cities go. Only about 10,000 inhabit its diminutive downtown, while the remaining two million populace reside in an area the size of a small New England state. As a result, a second car became a necessity. In Chicago, cars were, at best, a convenience, limited to grocery shopping or college football Saturday. But mostly, cars were a nuance, merely collecting dust and parking tickets.

Not coincidentally, the only person I spent time with in San Diego was gay. My affinity for gay men has nothing to do with sexuality and everything to do with personality. In short, my personality is considerably more gay than straight. Granted, I am a jock and readily accepted in straight circles. When it comes to deciding how I'm going to spend my free time, however, I choose to spend it with gay men for the simple reason that straight men are, by comparison, intolerably boring. Like gay men, I am playfully absurd, often histrionic, heading for the spotlight and center stage on the dance floor. I'm not gay. I'm bipolar, which mimics some gay behavior. In fact, for years I was fond of saying that I was raised, not by my parents, but by the "sexually ambiguous" Morrissey.

But this new friend was no Jeff, nor did I find a suitable Keith or Todd, for that matter. And San Diego was no Chicago. Though Michelle had considerably more friends in San Diego than I, she too, missed Chicago and her friends, who seemed much less like aliens than did the people in San Diego. By spring 1994, we decided to return to Chicago as soon as Michelle completed her graduate program that June.

In early July, we sold one car, rented another Ryder truck, hitched our remaining car to it, and headed northeast for Chicago. Upon arriving, we found an apartment on Irving Park Road and moved in right away. Though Todd was no longer around, having answered to higher callings – marriage and law school – our return to Chicago meant that four-fifths of the original core friends (Jeff, Michelle, Keith, and myself) was reunited. As always, Michelle found work right away, but not as a waitress. She was hired by one of the most prestigious law firms in Chicago as a paralegal.

Although her base salary was rather paltry, we never noticed. She soon became one of the most requested paralegals in the firm. As a result, almost two-thirds of her income was billed overtime.

With Michelle working long hours, Jeff and I resumed right where we had left off. In the fifteen months that I was away, Jeff had fully-reintegrated into the gay scene. The significance of this fact is that we spent several nights a week hopping from one gay bar or club to the next. For a straight guy with a girlfriend, this seemed like a terrific way to escape the self-obsessed rituals, pretentious self-importance, and unconcealed stalking that plagues straight clubs. Where straight clubs are all about one's hair — check and recheck endlessly — gay clubs are all about the show, and it's always showtime, baby!

I found work rather easily this time as a financial temporary. Every now and then, I would pursue permanent employment. However, that process was always doomed from the start. The simplest explanation for this is that I am an extremely difficult interview.

Q1: What are econometric models? I've never heard of this. I'm not certain that what we do here is all that clever.

Q2: So, let's see, you were 23 when you left California to enroll in a Ph.D. program in economics at the University of Illinois, where you received a handsome fellowship award. Then... you dropped out – how many times? Twice? Then you moved to Chicago and started working at a restaurant? Is this correct, you then moved to San Diego for fifteen months before returning to Chicago? And you've been a financial temp ever since? Did you get the chronology right, here, Mr. Pollard?

Q3: What are your hobbies, interests, etc., Mr. Pollard?

A1, A2, A3: *You can't handle the truth.*

Certainly, the interview is an act or performance for everyone. And yet, it's more so for me – to the point of distraction. I'm a horrible interview because of the following conflicting factors:

(a) There simply is not enough time in this process for the interviewer to get comfortable with me. Invariably, this process makes me defensive where I normally would not be. Most notably, consider the accomplishments and work experience I have omitted from my resume for fear of threatening the interviewer's sense of achievement. I refer to this phenomenon as the dumbing-down effect:

• Provided expert research and analysis in deriving the first econometric model to successfully demonstrate that the rapid expansion of U.S. financial markets in the 1980s has emerged as a dominant, exogenous factor in the recent determination of interest rates and the income velocity of money. An essay incorporating this model won a special merit award ($1,000) in the 1988 AMEX Bank Ltd. Review (London) *International Essay Competition* and was published by the Oxford University Press, 1989.

• Economic analyst specializing in econometrics, market concentrations, and economic damages. Project experience includes:

Specified an O.L.S. model to determine the economic damages suffered by a manufacturer as the result of the introduction and distribution by competitors of a product containing unique ingredients, the rights of which were held exclusively by the damaged party.

• Recipient of Proctor & Gamble Fellowship for Economics, 1989, from the University of Illinois at Urbana-Champaign; includes a $10,000 stipend and a full tuition waiver.

• Coping with a devastating mental illness finally diagnosed in 1991. This accounts for the seemingly reverse chronology and years of instability reflected on my resume. *(I have a mood disorder – I am not a felon.)*

Notably, all of the above occurred before my twenty-third birthday. The look of discomfort and bewilderment on the face of the interviewer at this stage of the process (i.e., the initial stage) invariably leaves me pondering these retorts: *I'm sorry you're not as smart as me,* or, *I'm sorry that you were much less ambitious at a similar age.*

(b) I know that the interviewer, like everyone, will grow to appreciate and genuinely like me over time;
(c) The interviewer is right about one thing: I am going to find this position boring, unchallenging, and unsatisfying – intolerably so.

In short, the interview is an awful process for me because it makes me feel anxious, ashamed, sheepish, inferior, defensive, inauthentic, angry, smug, arrogant, and superior. Ultimately, it asks me to accept stifling levels of both organizational and inter-office/interpersonal boredom. In the process, a necessary evil I call pruning occurs.

Even to the casual observer, I don't exactly resemble a square peg that slides neatly into the square hole. As a result, I figuratively, place myself in a box so as to both appear and sound employable. In other words, pruning is a form of compliance that employs artificial constraints. Invariably, this act places me in a catch-22. Once I submit to the pruning, the question becomes how long can I last before I grow intolerant of myself, of everyone, and of everything around me?

By contrast, temping, a form of underemployment, at least gives me the opportunity to freelance. And in this way, I am responsible for maintaining my interest level. But that's nothing new to me. Psychotherapy has shown me that I've been solely responsible for maintaining my interest level (more specifically, for managing the intolerable, restless irritability that accompanies boredom) since childhood, when I was developing board games by the age of 9 or 10.

Inconceivably, both our core friends remained inseparable and our lives kept moving right along, without incident, through 1994, 1995, and 1996. It doesn't take a psychiatrist to deduce that I must have been taking my medication during this period of remarkable stability. But that didn't prevent information from being translated into particularly dangerous thinking. The following trap has only recently been brought to light through the aid of psychotherapy.

Fact 1: I certainly accept that I am bipolar.

Fact 2: By definition, I am susceptible to profound mood swings in either direction.

Fact 3: I have an extensive knowledge base to draw from.

Fact 4: I specifically take medication to avoid these harrowing mood swings.

Fact 5: I have not experienced a troublesome mood swing since returning to lithium, a mood stabilizer, in the spring of 1993.

Misinterpretation of the facts: *Now on lithium, I have completely eradicated undesirable mood swings.*

Today, I am beginning to recognize more subtle, yet very significant, mood swings that pack all of the destructive force of the more grand forms.

By 1996, Michelle and I had been through many galvanizing experiences together and fully expected to marry. All that needed to be worked out were a few of the details. I was against having children; initially, she was, too. But for her, that was beginning to change. Also, I wanted to elope; she wanted a traditional church wedding, and all that goes with it.

The first kink in the armor appeared when Michelle began experimenting with the notion of motherhood. For me, one of Michelle's most charming qualities is that she has no maternal sense or instinct, whatsoever. This is no harsh criticism. Rather, considering the source, it is a gushing compliment. (No, that comment didn't make things any better.) Eventually, this experiment manifested itself in the acquisition of pets.

One glorious spring morning, Michelle and I packed the car and set out for a camping expedition in Wisconsin. But before we had traveled ten blocks, Michelle directed me to a favorite pet shop of hers. There was no thwarting it now. The gestation period elapsed. Motherhood had arrived, and we were about to become the proud parents of a kitten. Six hundred dollars later, we left the store with a car full of accessories and an adorable, eleven-pound basset hound puppy.

Immediately, Michelle named him Irving, in honor of our home on Irving Park Road. And so the great experiment was on, giving me ample opportunity to note that Michelle simply was not cut out for motherhood. After about a year of this phase of the experiment, Michelle attributed her alleged shortcomings to the fact that she had wanted a kitten in the first place. By early 1997, I was in favor of adding a kitten to the household if nothing more than to keep Irving company. Back to the pet store. Boris, a tiny orange tabby kitten, took to his new brother, a gentle-giant, right away.

By August, it was clear that phase two of the experiment was not going that much better. In what I thought would put an end to this discussion for good, Michelle admitted that her motherly instincts for our animals were, indeed, deficient. "But," she added, "I think I will be a good mother to my own children." That sealed my fate. By September 1997, Irving and I had moved to nearby Bittersweet Place, while Michelle and Boris remained at Irving Park Road.

Chapter 4
KEITH'S WATCH

If staying alive is a desirable thing, then Jeff, Michelle, and Keith are most responsible for making this so for me. By the time Michelle and I had split up, Jeff was enjoying the fruits of romantic love, at long last. As a result, he, like Michelle, was virtually unavailable. Incredibly, Keith emerged to fill the void left by the others. In fact, "Keith's watch" as my lookout continues to this day. Keith doesn't claim to understand me. Nor does he care to engage me as I rip off on some tirade at any given moment, as I am want to do from time to time. Instead, Keith employs a disarming technique that exploits my propensity toward distractibility. Da Bears! Poker! Tennis!

Fearful that my break-up with Michelle would plunge me into a major depressive episode, I did a very smart thing and requested to see a therapist from my community mental health center. Much to my amazement, however, I never detected a significant mood swing. This finding, therefore, further reinforced my earlier misinterpretation that as long as I continued to take medication, troublesome mood swings would be completely eradicated. More precisely, the last time that I had detected a significant mood swing occurred after I had stopped taking my medication in early 1993. From that point forward, I have remained medication compliant. Little did I know that two-and-a half years would pass before the folly of my working model was exposed.

The next time I detected a significant mood swing wasn't until late 2000. Like mania, stability has a seductive feature to it. For all intents and purposes, my negligence here is akin to that of a driver who nods off at the wheel during the course of a routine drive home, a drive negotiated successfully hundreds of times over the years. In short, there exists an inverse relationship between the driver's familiarity with the task at hand and his or her attentiveness. In either case, the destructive force that unfolds is often profound, while the effects can be long lasting. Having said that, I stopped seeing the therapist after just three sessions.

The move to Bittersweet placed me at the center of the dog owning community, Dog Park. Dog Park is many things to many people. But to some of us, it is adult high school, twice a day, seven days a week. Greg, Luis, and I are somewhat patriarchs of Dog Park and have been meeting regularly since the fall of 1997. Together, we formed a small, all-male click and flirted with every mommy who dared venture near. Though juvenile, our technique proved remarkably effective, nonetheless. I have dated two mommies, nearly married one, and Greg is presently engaged to marry another. Additionally, by mid-fall of 1997 Michelle and I had become the best of friends once again. We talked freely and frankly, as we still do, about everything from our pets and families to our current relationships.

After Michelle, I did not enter another serious relationship until November 1998, when I began dating my future ex-fiancé. She was one of the Dog Park mommies that I had invited into my circle. Like Michelle, she too was a strikingly attractive, young woman. She had come to Chicago to study psychology, a subject that I had grown increasingly interested in in recent years. Initially, she was both scared and in awe of me and admitted this much.

Shortly after we began dating, I had fulfilled a life's dream by visiting London. A curious footnote: my mother's invitation to join the family for Thanksgiving in San Francisco compelled me to go to London, instead. Immediately after declining her invitation, I booked a flight to England. I told myself, *I'll deal with accommodations when I get there.* As it turned out, London was swamped with Christmas shoppers from various parts of Europe. Consequently, all affordable rooms were booked until the next day. *No problem, I'll simply put my small backpack in a locker at a nearby train stop and walk the streets of London for 26 consecutive hours, mingling with interesting people along the way.* I did not mind this inconvenience one bit. In fact, experiences like this have left me critical of those who rely so heavily on prepackaged travel accommodations.

> *Excuse me, but where is the fun, the challenge, the socialization, or the sense of adventure in all of that? Pardon me, but your tour guide is being paid to talk to you, and the folks around you are from the Midwest*

*and New England. Are you afraid you'd forget to visit
the Buckingham Palace unless your chaperone drives
you there? Come on!*

All right, so criticism accompanies hypomania. And, admittedly, it does help to be, at the very least, hypomanic, when asked to walk the streets of a strange city for 26 consecutive hours.

In addition to all of the obvious sights one hopes to see when in London, I had included a few more: Freud's home at one end of town, Wimbledon at the far reaches of the other end, and the centrally located Sloane Square and Piccadilly Circus. These last two stops were included expressly because Morrissey had sung about them. Given time considerations, however, other lyrically referenced neighborhoods, such as Vauxhall and Arsenal, seemed less alluring.

A few weeks after returning from London, I visited my new girlfriend and her family over the Christmas holiday. For various reasons, she pleaded with me to let her out, concluding that I would not like her because she was too boring for me. At the time, I didn't have enough information about her to fully appreciate what she had just told me. Later, however, I would come to interpret this plea as her way of telling me that she's the kind of person who insisted on purchasing prepackaged tours and traveling with her family.

At any rate, we had been dating for only a month. Besides that, I had just driven through a major blizzard from Chicago to Buffalo to join her and her family over her Christmas break. I was feeling happy and believed that she contributed to my happiness. Moreover, I wanted her to know that it was safe to freak-out in front of me. At the same time, I felt comforted by the notion that she, a doctorate student of psychology, accepted me, bipolar and all.

A bittersweet (noun) happens to be a woody plant. Just like a bittersweet's vine, my wayward shoots are subject to pruning each time I enter a relationship. This phenomenon is analogous to that which occurs during the interview process and for all the same reasons. Recall, the interview process presents me with this catch-22. Once I submit to the pruning, the question becomes how long can I last before I grow intolerant of myself, of everyone, and of everything around me? Relationships are no different. The relationship trap goes like this:

If, on one hand, I don't prune away a good portion of my spirit, then I can't be with the one I love. But once I submit to the pruning, the question becomes how long can I last before I grow intolerant of myself, of everyone, and of everything around me?

Make no mistake, this is neither projection nor catastrophizing. Pruning is necessary because, as with the financial world, I don't fit neatly into some socially acceptable slot. This has always been and will remain a problem for significant others to come.

Hi mom and dad. I have a new boyfriend. Well... he's a lot of fun, relatively unemployable, not fond of family, and really smart!

The danger herein is that, when stripped of too much of my spirit, I begin to lose heart. This simple statement has two major implications. The first, unless I submit to a necessary amount of pruning, I will be alone. The second, I have no way to measure my spirit so as to clip off an appropriate amount. It then becomes a guessing game, and I submit to some pruning, then a little more, then more again, and again to the point that I grow intolerant of myself, of everyone around me, and of everything. Learned helplessness theory describes this phenomenon as one struggles against pruning, but eventually submits, relinquishing more and more control in the process. Ultimately, the individual grows depressed.

I am certain that this was precisely what occurred between my ex-fiancé and myself. Suddenly, what was important to me was so no longer. Moreover, it had been replaced by what was important to her: children, a large engagement ring, a traditional church wedding, and moving away from Chicago. But that couldn't possibly be long lasting. A life's experience has shown that my drive toward wholeness is dominant, inconveniently at the expense of both employability and relationships, alike.

My ex-fiancé was many things, but chief among them was that she was an astute student of psychology. Had it not been for her, I never would have seen the need for psychotherapy. Additionally, she was the first to challenge my working model: as long as I continue to take my medication, my troublesome mood swings have been completely eradicated. Eventually, her accusation just days before moving out led me to the DSM-IV (a reference manual for use in psychiatric diagnosis) and a discussion of *hypomania* and *mixed states.*

By January 2000, Keith's role as my lookout had expanded from playing endless hours of poker with me, to talking to the police (who had responded to a 9-1-1 call from my apartment), and providing me refuge on his couch. Meanwhile, I had begun seeing a psychotherapist referred by my ex-fiancé.

While my tumultuous engagement both rapidly and acrimoniously deteriorated, I continued to work as a financial temp and was finishing up an internship with a substance abuse treatment center. Since the late 1980s, when I participated in a family intervention, I was mesmerized by the family systems approach to dysfunctional families in general, and the information I had learned about myself in particular. As a result, I was convinced that someday I might gravitate toward this field. Much to my surprise, by the end of my internship, I was offered a position as a therapist at this treatment center, effective immediately.

Suddenly and unexpectedly, I found myself at a crossroads. On the one hand, if I passed on this offer, (lacking proper credentials) I was not likely to find comparable work in a suitable environment. Moreover, having already cancelled the wedding by this time, there was reason to believe that we may never marry. If indeed that was the case, I would feel like an even bigger fool should I pass on this offer. Besides, if my fiancé really wanted to be with me, she would be supportive. If, on the other hand, I accepted this position, and the accompanying pay cut ($10,000 per annum), my fiancé was going to flip. All things considered, I accepted the offer at the end of April. By mid-June, my ex-fiancé had moved out.

In September 2000, the first sign of trouble surfaced at the treatment center. During a staff meeting, I questioned the Director of Operations about our use of staff meeting time, suggesting that we should use it to plan for foreseeable events, such as the absence of two-fifths of our therapeutic staff due to vacation. Two unsettling incidents followed this suggestion. First, the director ended the discussion by barking at me, "Get over it!" Second, my colleagues said nothing during the staff meeting, but afterward commended me for standing up to the director, adding, "that's why we stopped asking for help years ago!"

By March 2001, however, I had been besieged by a number of negative life experiences. In October 2000, I filed for bankruptcy. Student loans, underemployment and periods of unemployment, more than a decade without health insurance and medical bills that went unpaid, out-of-pocket payments for the treatment of mental illness, a career change and its accompanying pay cut, and, finally, a costly engagement, both personally and financially, ultimately conspired against me.

That Thanksgiving I flew home (to San Francisco) to see my eight-month-old-nephew for the first time, only to discover that his lingering cold was, in fact, spinal meningitis. As a result, he had been placed in an intensive care unit the day before my arrival. He would be in and out of intensive care from Thanksgiving to Christmas, as his meningitis was complicated by hydrocephalus, before returning home, relatively carefree and with a shunt in his skull to allow fluid to drain.

Upon returning to Chicago, my therapist and I realized that I had been overcome by profound sorrow. We attributed it to the time of the year (winter), my untimely visit with my sick nephew, and the succession of personal and professional struggles that had recently devoured my serenity. In response to a depressive interval, my history is ancient: I respond, as I have since childhood, with efforts to reassert myself. Interestingly, this drive ultimately manifested itself in the form of this memoir. In the meantime, however, I directed my energies to a less noble attack on my ex-fiancé.

By January 2001, in an attempt to distract myself from dwelling over my single status, I decided to start dating. But after just the third date, I became harshly critical and intolerant of virtually everything about that young woman. Rather than sharing all that I had found unappealing about her, I decided to leave her alone, instead. Though the dating had successfully distracted me for a few weeks, in the end, it left me feeling more irritable, more restless, and more critical of everyone and everything around me. So I began taking very long walks through a frozen city, stopping along the way to catch a movie or a band, or anything that suggested it could help me to better manage my depression. A major appeal of city life, especially true of Chicago and New York, is that it offers various outlets to help one manage both depression and mania, alike.

Next, I turned harshly critical of my roommate, who I had suspected was taking advantage of my willingness to walk his dog throughout the winter months. But Irving's sudden change in health quickly trumped that outrage, for the moment, anyway. Irving began bedwetting and I franticly searched for an inexpensive explanation.

By the end of February, things at the treatment center grew increasingly more surreal each day. For a number of reasons, namely, that my clinical supervisor had resigned two months earlier, that the director did not intend to replace her (not already certified, I alone required clinical supervision), and that I was growing increasingly disgruntled with my director's management style, I decided to take steps toward resigning. First, I revisited the equitability of workloads issue that I had first introduced in September.

Only this time, I left no stones uncovered. I did the math for my director.

To make my point clear, which should always be one's design when constructing an argument, in an innocuous memo I compared my actual workload (staff maximum) to that of a coworker's (staff minimum) for the month of February 2001. I also attached a self-explanatory spreadsheet supporting my findings and suggested that the director himself may need to intervene to reconcile this disparity. Then, I waited for his response. The response was immediate. However, it came from an unlikely source: the coworker named in the memo.

Unannounced, my coworker burst into my office and, noticeably agitated, began to explain that while she was working in the director's office, she saw my memo lying on his desk. Upon noticing her name in it, she decided to read it and grew infuriated with me, saying that I had accused her of being lazy. To make an ugly story short, I first pointed out that my memo was not intended for her to read and mentioned that it was in fact innocuous – it merely suggested that the director get more involved on the unit to make things equitable – before firing back at her: "Get the fuck out of my office!" That coworker resigned the following day. Despite her assurance to all that I was not responsible for her decision to resign, the director made it clear at the next staff meeting, however, that he begged to differ.

In any event, I continued to wait for the director's response to my memo. None was forthcoming, however, so I decided to draft a letter of my easily remedied grievances to the attention of the C.E.O. Working with my therapist, I wrote and rewrote a well-argued letter that not only identified a number of problematic developments on the unit, but suggested ways to remedy them, as well.

After an entire week had passed and the director had yet to respond, I resolved to take this matter to the C.E.O. One rare afternoon, I found the C.E.O. in his office and proceeded to enter. Upon explaining the nature of the matter to him, he suggested that I take it up with the director, to which I replied, "Yeah, I did that last week. He won't address it. My thinking is, I need you to ask him to look at this stuff." Until that point, the director simply lacked sufficient incentive to consider my grievances. After all, collectively, they amounted to a complete indictment on him for his lack of leadership on the unit.

Interestingly, by the following staff meeting the director had indeed found the impetus to address my letter writing. True to form, however, he did so in an underhanded way. To open the meeting, rather than making my grievances public, he began a methodical, piecemeal attack of my arguments, attempting to discredit me in front of my colleagues. By design, the director and I were the only parties privy to the information being discussed, and thus my colleagues were reduced to the role of onlookers to a street fight.

His approach to most things may seem mysterious to some, but to me, it was highly conspicuous. Keep the rank and file in the dark about everything; in this way, they were more inclined to accept what they were told without challenge. My case, however, was different. Assuredly, as history predicted, I was going down in flames.

Over the course of the next hour, I proceeded to accuse the director of, among other things, introducing red herrings into the discussion so as to confuse the issues and of hiding behind a worthless piece of paper and its irrelevant numbers simply because experience has taught him that he could get away with it. Additionally, I placed the blame for the staff resignation on the director's lack of leadership and charged that the director had left my memo on his desk deliberately for this staff member (who occasionally worked out of the director's office) to read. "That sort of blew up in your face, didn't it?"

Bigmouth strikes again!

Indeed, I was terminated. My last tie to the treatment center, then, was obtaining my final paycheck. I was let go on March 6 and by March 21, despite repeated assurances that the check had been mailed, I was prepared to take matters into my own hands. Instead, I did something a lot more rational. I called Keith, explained my predicament, and then asked if he would accompany me to the treatment center to ensure that things don't get out of hand.

"I don't like the way this is going, and by now I'm expecting the worst from these clowns. Your job is

to beat me off of them should I reach for someone's throat."

With Keith onboard, I informed the controller that I would
stop by in ten minutes to pick up my check. I also instructed him to have it waiting for me. Fortunately, the check was
delivered to me in the main lobby in a timely fashion, and
Keith and I had a quiet lunch together shortly thereafter.

Chapter 5
BITTERSWEET

I wrote this bittersweet memoir in the wake of the latest destructive depressive episode, from the now familiar position of my newly unemployed bum, in the living room of my lovely, vintage apartment located, appropriately enough, on Bittersweet Place. In one sense, this memoir can be seen as nothing more than an ancient ritual acted out in response to depression. In another sense, it could be seen as the fruit of my sabbatical.

All agree that the human being is flawed, but just what exactly are we agreeing to? The sexual indiscretions of a president? We may point to that as being an example of a flawed human being. In this model, however, it is important to note that sexual indiscretion is a forgivable flaw simply because it falls within the common experience we associate with being human.

Mental illness, by contrast, is not forgivable. For various reasons, the experiences of the mentally ill are not recognized as human experiences. Wish as we may that the human being is not too badly flawed, reality suggests otherwise: it is often warped, demented, and even grotesque.

This discussion brings me back to a conversation I had at Dog Park. One afternoon a friend approached me, appalled by the story he was about to share.

> Can you believe this? Some asshole knocked on my neighbor's door – she's this little old lady – and when she came to answer it, he knocked her down, beat her up, and stole $30 from her purse. Can you believe that? I mean, this guy's not human, he's an animal!

Having experienced mental illness firsthand and having worked with a drug abusing mentally ill population for more than a year, I merely shrugged and offered these possible explanations: "He's probably a drug addict, mentally ill, or both."

Where is the wonder in my friend's story? Here, the scoundrel is said to be an animal. The fact is, neither an animal, nor a fish, nor a tree, for that matter, assaulted this woman – a human being did. Had it, in fact, been an animal, wonder would then be fitting. My claim is that the only way to account for my friend's astonishment here, and our nation's in general, is to recognize the unrealistically narrow range of experiences we label human experiences. Can this scoundrel be said to be flawed? Absolutely. If, indeed, this man is mentally ill, are his flaws forgivable? Absolutely not. In other words, no man may be too flawed. And therein lies the horror of a friend over a robbery at one end, and of a nation over high school gunmen at the other.

In the final verse of "The Boy with the Thorn in His Side," Morrissey begs the question, "Who do you need to know?" To the subject of childhood depression, the answer is resounding: mental health professionals – counselors, social workers, therapists, and psychiatrists. Why mental health professionals? Simple. They are trained to deal with the unpleasant subject of mental illness. Moreover, unlike my friend, they've seen it all before, and therefore don't find the subject all that remarkable. In other words, one is not likely to send a mental health professional into a fit of denial: "Come on, you don't really mean that, do you? You know, a lot of people feel the blues every now and then – I'm sure you're just normal. Besides, you probably just had a bit too much to drink."

Imagine being my psychiatrist during the summer of 1991. Imagine having to listen to the same arrogant, often pious, and always incessant ranting, three days a week, disputing everything that your profession has to say about this illness. Imagine me, your patient, refusing to take medication, dismissing you as being bookish, and repeating my claim that it is normal for me to feel as though I have metaphysical powers. And yet, nothing that I did or said ever shocked, delighted, encouraged, or disappointed my psychiatrist.

To help illustrate my point, consider the following two scenarios. The first is a discussion between a parent, prone to fits of denial, and a child. The second examines the matter of who receives treatment for childhood depression.

Scenario I

Parent: What do you mean you want to blow up the town? You know, we picked this town because we wanted the best for you kids. Besides, most people would love to live in our tranquil community. Now, why on earth would you want to do a thing like that?
Child: Because I hate this town, I hate you, and I hate myself.
Parent: You watch your mouth. I just don't know what to do with you.

One might expect that the child here had to watch his or her mouth regularly, and that the parent really didn't know what to do with the irreverent child. Specifically, the parent didn't know that there was cause for considering childhood depression and, more importantly, for taking the child to see a mental health professional.

Now, consider a more demonstrative case of childhood depression, the presenting childhood symptoms, and the implications for treatment.

Scenario II

Patient: child
Age: 10
Presenting Symptoms as a Child: wish to die, suicide attempt
Childhood Treatment: given psychiatric evaluation and treatment immediately following suicide attempt

Sadly, the child from Scenario I may happen upon mal-adaptive ways of coping with childhood depression that are both horrific and self-destructive.

As has been discussed at length, the only seemingly positive or constructive response to a horrible illness lands a child in an impossible catch-22, one that is built into a society that does not understand mental illness as being along the same continuum labeled human experience. It can thus be argued that achievement is nothing more than an adaptive response to depression. Specifically, through achievement, the distraction of activity and the reinforcement through reward allow a child, only momentarily, to escape the profound sorrow and self-loathing.

This, then, begs the following question: what exactly is commendable and worth reinforcing? The answer is disturbing: apparently, a child's ill-fated attempt to cope with depression is worth reinforcing. Finally, Scenario II exposes another equally unfortunate outcome. When intervention does occur, it does so too late for a nation (childhood gunmen), too late for a family (Scenario II), and too late for an individual (Scenario I).

Before handing me the "Most Inspirational Player Award," my high school football coach introduced me to the audience in this way. This is not an attempt to single out my coach; I made many adults think this about me:

"I want my son to grow up to be just like Marc Pollard."

Wow, coach, you must really hate your son.